GEMS FROM
TOZER

GEMS FROM
TOZER

Selections from the writings

of

A. W. TOZER

CHRISTIAN PUBLICATIONS

Camp Hill, Pennsylvania

U.S. edition by permission
of
Send The Light Trust—1979
Christian Publications
3825 Hartzdale Drive, Camp Hill, PA 17011
ISBN 0-87509-163-6

CONTENTS

THE KNOWLEDGE AND PURSUIT OF THE MOST HIGH

The gradual disappearance of the idea and feeling of majesty from the Church is a sign and a portent. Our God has now become our servant to wait on our will. "The Lord is *my shepherd*," we say, instead of "*The Lord* is my shepherd," and the difference is as wide as the world.   2

The Church has surrendered her once lofty concept of God and has substituted for it one so low, so ignoble, as to be utterly unworthy of thinking, worshipping men.

The low view of God entertained almost universally among Christians is the cause of a hundred lesser evils everywhere among us. A whole new philosophy of the Christian life has resulted from this one basic error in our religious thinking.   3

The world is perishing for lack of the knowledge of God and the Church is famishing for want of His Presence.   6

To most people God is an inference, not a reality. He is a deduction from evidence which they consider adequate, but He remains personally unknown to the individual. For millions of Christians God is no more real than He is to the non-Christian.

Over against all this cloudy vagueness stands the clear Scriptural doctrine that God can be known in personal experience. A loving Personality dominates the Bible.

But why do the very ransomed children of God know so little of that habitual conscious communion with God which the Scriptures seem to offer? The answer is our chronic unbelief. God and the spiritual world are real. But sin has so clouded the lenses of our hearts that we cannot see. The great unseen Reality is God.

As we begin to focus upon God the things of the spirit will take shape before our inner eyes. Obedience to the word of Christ will bring an inward revelation of the Godhead (John 14:21-23). A new God-consciousness will seize upon us and we shall begin to taste and hear and inwardly feel the God who is our life and our all. God will become to us the great All, and His Presence the glory and wonder of our lives. 6

In Christ and by Christ, God effects complete self-disclosure, although He shows Himself not to reason but to faith and love. Faith is an organ of knowledge, and love an organ of experience. God came to us in the incarnation; in atonement He reconciled us to Himself, and by faith and love we enter and lay hold on Him. 3

Love and faith are at home in the mystery of the Godhead. Let reason kneel in reverence outside. 3

Satan's first attack upon the human race was his sly effort to destroy Eve's confidence in the kindness of God. From that day, men have had a false conception of God. Nothing twists and deforms the soul more than a low or unworthy conception of God. The God of the Pharisees was not a God easy to live with.

From a failure properly to understand God comes a world of unhappiness among good Christians even today. The Christian life is thought to be a glum, unrelieved cross-carrying under the eye of a stern Father who expects much and excuses nothing. The truth is that God is the most winsome of all beings and His service one of unspeakable pleasure. He loves us for ourselves and values our love more than galaxies of new created worlds.

Unfortunately many Christians cannot get free from their perverted notions of God, and these notions poison their hearts and destroy their inward freedom. These friends serve God grimly, as the elder brother did, doing what is right without enthusiasm and without joy.

How good it would be if we could learn that God is easy to live with. 7

God has not bowed to our nervous haste nor embraced the methods of our machine age. *The man who would know God must give time to Him.* 2

All of God's acts are consistent with all of His attributes. All that God does agrees with all that God is, and being and doing are one in Him. He cannot act out of character with Himself.

I think it might be demonstrated that almost every heresy that has afflicted the church through the years has arisen from believing about God things that are not true, or from over-emphasizing certain true things so as to obscure other things equally true. To magnify any attribute to the exclusion of another is to head straight for one of the dismal swamps of theology, and yet we are all constantly tempted to do just that.

For instance, the Bible teaches that God is love; some have interpreted this in such a way as virtually to deny that He is just, which the Bible also teaches. Others press the Biblical doctrine of God's goodness so far that it is made to contradict His holiness. Or they make His compassion cancel out His truth. Still others understand the sovereignty of God in a way that destroys or at least greatly diminishes His goodness and love.

We can hold a correct view of truth only by daring to believe everything God has said about Himself. It is a grave responsibility that a man takes upon himself when he seeks to edit out of God's self-revelation such features as he in his ignorance deems objectionable. 3

The Persons of the Godhead never work separately. Every act of God is done by all three Persons. 2

What peace it brings to the Christian's heart to realize that our Heavenly Father never differs from Himself. In coming to Him at any time we need not wonder whether we shall find Him in a receptive mood. He is always receptive to misery and need, as well as to love and faith. He does not keep office hours nor set aside periods when He will see no one. Neither does He change His mind about anything. God never changes moods or cools off in His affections or loses enthusiasm.

God will not compromise and He need not be coaxed. He cannot be persuaded to alter His Word nor talked into answering selfish prayer. In all our efforts to find God, to please Him, to commune with Him, we should remember that all change must be on our part. "I am the Lord, I change not." We have but to meet His clearly stated terms, bring our lives into accord with His revealed will, and His infinite power will become instantly operative toward us in the manner set forth through the gospel in the Scriptures of truth. 3

"I am that I am," says God, "I change not." As the sailor locates his position on the sea by "shooting" the sun, so we may get our moral bearings by looking at God. We must begin with God.

Much of our difficulty as seeking Christians stems from our unwillingness to take God as He is and adjust our lives accordingly. We insist upon trying to modify Him and to bring Him nearer to our own image. The flesh whimpers against the rigor of God's inexorable sentence and begs like Agag for a little mercy, a little indulgence of its carnal ways. It is no use. We can get a right start only by accepting God as He is and learning to love Him for what He is. As we go on to know Him better we shall find it a source of unspeakable joy that God is just what He is. 6

How completely satisfying to turn from our limitations to a God who has none. Eternal years lie in His heart. For Him time does not pass, it remains; and those who are in Christ share with Him all the riches of limitless time and endless years. God never hurries. There are no deadlines against which He must work. Only to know this is to quiet our spirits and relax our nerves. For those out of Christ, time is a devouring beast.

The Christian man possesses God's own life and shares His infinitude with Him. In God there is life enough for all and time enough to enjoy it. His love is boundless.   3

If faith is the gaze of the heart at God, and if this gaze is but the raising of the inward eyes to meet the all-seeing eyes of God, then it follows that it is one of the easiest things possible to do. It would be like God to make the most vital thing easy and place it within the range of possibility for the weakest and poorest of us.   6

To know God is at once the easiest and the most difficult thing in the world. It is easy because the knowledge is not won by hard mental toil, but is something freely given. As sunlight falls on the open field, so the knowledge of the holy God is a free gift to men who are open to receive it. But this knowledge is difficult because there are conditions to be met and the obstinate nature of fallen man does not take kindly to them.   3

The Christian conception of God current in these middle years of the twentieth-century is so decadent as to be utterly beneath the dignity of the Most High God and actually to constitute for professed believers something amounting to a moral calamity.

With our loss of the sense of majesty has come the further loss of religious awe and consciousness of the divine Presence. We have lost our spirit of worship and our ability to withdraw inwardly to meet God in adoring silence.   3

THE MISSING JEWEL
OF WORSHIP

We are called to an everlasting preoccupation with God. 8

God is spirit and they that worship Him must worship Him in spirit and in truth. Only the Holy Spirit can enable a fallen man to worship God acceptably. As far as that's concerned, only the Holy Spirit can pray acceptably; only the Holy Spirit can do anything acceptably. 15

Man was made to worship God. God gave man a harp and said, "Here above all the creatures that I have made and created I have given you the largest harp. . .you can worship Me in a manner that no other creature can." And when he sinned man took that instrument and threw it down in the mud. 15

Why did Christ come? In order that He might make worshippers out of rebels. We were created to worship. Worship is the normal employment of moral beings. Worship is a moral imperative. Worship is the missing jewel in modern evangelicalism.

I want to define worship, and here is where I

want to be dogmatic. Worship means "to feel in the heart." A person that merely goes through the form and does not feel anything is not worshipping.

Worship also means to "express in some appropriate manner" what you feel. And what will be expressed? "A humbling but delightful sense of admiring awe and astonished wonder." It is delightful to worship God, but it is also a humbling thing.

Now what are the factors that you will find present in worship? First there is *boundless confidence*. You cannot worship a Being you cannot trust. Then there is *admiration*, that is, appreciation of the excellency of God. *Fascination* is another element in true worship; to be filled with moral excitement; to be captivated and charmed and entranced with who God is, and struck with astonished wonder at the inconceivable elevation and magnitude and splendor of Almighty God. Next is *adoration*; to love God with all the power within us; to love God with fear and wonder and yearning and awe. At times this will lead us to breathless silence. 15

The God of the modern evangelical rarely astonishes anybody. He manages to stay pretty much within the constitution. Never breaks over our bylaws. He's a very well-behaved God and very denominational and very much one of us, and we ask Him to help us when we're in trouble and look to Him to watch over us when we're asleep. The God of the modern evangelical isn't a God I could have much respect for. But when the Holy Ghost shows us God as He is we admire Him to the point of wonder and delight. 15

Worship. . .rises or falls with our concept of God; that is why I do not believe in these half-converted cowboys who call God the Man Upstairs. I do not think they worship at all because their concept of God is unworthy of God and unworthy of them. And if there is one terrible disease in the Church of Christ, it is that we do not see God as great as He is. We're too familiar with God.   15

Worship is pure or base as the worshipper entertains high or low thoughts of God. We tend by a secret law of the soul to move toward our mental image of God.   3

We're here to be worshippers first and workers only second. We take a convert and immediately make a worker out of him. God never meant it to be so. God meant that a convert should learn to be a worshipper, and after that he can learn to be a worker. The work done by a worshipper will have eternity in it.   15

Labor that does not spring out of worship is futile and can only be wood, hay and stubble in the day that shall try every man's works.   1

It is rarely that we find anyone aglow with personal love for Christ. This love as a kind of moral fragrance is ever detected upon the garments of the saints. The list of fragrant saints is long. It includes men and women of every shade of theological thought within the bounds of the orthodox Christian faith. This radiant love for Christ is to my mind the true test of catholicity, the one sure proof of membership in the church universal.   8

MAN CREATED TO BE
THE DWELLING PLACE
OF GOD

Deep inside every man there is a private sanctum where dwells the mysterious essence of his being. This far-in reality is that in the man which is what it is of itself, without reference to any other part of the man's complex nature. It is the man's "I am," a gift from the I AM who created him.

The deep-in human entity of which we speak is called in the Scriptures *the spirit of man,* (1 Cor. 2:11). As God's self-knowledge lies in the eternal Spirit, so man's self-knowledge is by his own spirit, and his knowledge of God is by the direct impression of the Spirit of God upon the spirit of man. The importance of all this cannot be overestimated as we think and study and pray.

From man's standpoint the most tragic loss suffered in the Fall was the vacating of this inner sanctum by the Spirit of God. There God planned to rest and glow with moral and spiritual fire. Man by his sin forfeited this indescribably wonderful privilege and must now dwell there alone.

By the mysterious operation of the Spirit in the

new birth, that which is called by Peter "the divine nature" enters the deep-in core of the believer's heart and establishes residence there. Such a one is a true Christian, and only such. 4

An infinite God can give all of Himself to each of His children. He does not distribute Himself that each may have a part, but to each one He gives all of Himself as fully as if there were no others. 2

One cause of the decline in the quality of religious experience among Christians these days is the neglect of the doctrine of the inward witness.

One distinguishing mark of those first Christians was a supernatural radiance that shined out from within them. The sun had come up in their hearts and its warmth and light made unnecessary any secondary sources of assurance. They had the inner witness. It is obvious that the average evangelical Christian today is without this radiance. Instead of the inner witness we now substitute logical conclusions drawn from texts. 1

The world's own prophets, the unbelieving psychologists (those eyeless seekers who seek for a light which is not God's light) have been forced to recognize at the bottom of religious experience this sense of *something there*. But better far is the sense of *Someone there*. It was this that filled with abiding wonder the first members of the Church of Christ. The solemn delight which those early disciples knew sprang straight from the conviction that there was One in the midst of them. How wonderful is this sense of Someone there. It makes religion invulnerable to critical attack. It secures the mind against collapse under the battering of the enemy. They who worship the

18

God who is present may ignore the objections of unbelieving men. What they see and hear overwhelms their doubts and confirms their assurance beyond the power of argument to destroy. Nothing can take the place of the *touch* of God in the soul and the sense of Someone there. Where true faith is, the knowledge of God will be given as a fact of consciousness altogether apart from the conclusions of logic. The spiritual giants of old *experienced God.* 2

We are only now emerging from a long ice age during which an undue emphasis was laid upon objective truth at the expense of subjective experience.

Wise leaders should have known that the human heart cannot exist in a vacuum. If Christians are forbidden to enjoy the wine of the Spirit they will turn to the wine of the flesh for enjoyment. Our teachers took away our right to be happy in God and the human heart wreaked its terrible vengeance by going on a fleshly binge from which the evangelical Church will not soon recover, if indeed it ever does. Christ died for our hearts and the Holy Spirit wants to come and satisfy them. 7

One quality belonging to the Holy Spirit, of great interest and importance to every seeking heart, is penetrability. He can penetrate matter, such as the human body; He can penetrate mind; He can penetrate another spirit such as the human spirit. He can achieve complete penetration of and actual inter-mingling with the human spirit. He can invade the human heart and make room for Himself without expelling anything essentially human. The integrity of the human personality remains unimpaired. Only moral evil is forced to withdraw. 2

A man by his sin may waste himself, which is to waste that which on earth is most like God. This is man's greatest tragedy, God's heaviest grief.

Sin has many sides and many ramifications. It is like a disease with numberless complications, any one of which can kill the patient. It is lawlessness, it is a missing of the mark, it is rebellion, it is perversion, it is transgression; but it is also waste—a frightful, tragic waste of the most precious of all treasures. The man who dies out of Christ is said to be lost, and hardly a word in the English tongue expresses his condition with greater accuracy. He has squandered a rare fortune and at the last he stands for a fleeting moment and looks around, a moral fool, a wastrel who has lost in one overwhelming and irrecoverable loss, his soul, his life, his peace, his total, mysterious personality, his dear and everlasting all. 7

When God infuses eternal life into the spirit of a man, the man becomes a member of a new and higher order of being. 3

We who live in this nervous age would be wise to meditate on our lives and our days long and often before the face of God and on the edge of eternity. For we are made for eternity as certainly as we are made for time. To be made for eternity and forced to dwell in time is for mankind a tragedy of huge proportions. All within us cries for life and permanence, and everything around us reminds us of mortality and change. Yet that God has made us of the stuff of eternity is both a glory and a prophecy.

Just here the sweet relevancy of the Christian message appears. "Jesus Christ...hath abolished death, and hath brought life and immortality to light through the gospel." For every man it must be Christ or eternal tragedy. Out of eternity our Lord came into time to rescue his human brethren whose moral folly had made them not only fools of the passing world but slaves of sin and death as well. 3

What is the supreme benefaction, the gift and treasure above all others which even God can give? He gives Christ to be in our nature forever. This is God's supreme and final gift. Not the pearly gates, not the golden streets, not heaven, not even the forgiveness of sins, although these are God's gifts too. Not a dozen, or two dozen, or a thousand, but countless hundreds of thousands of gifts God lays before His happy people, and then bestows this supreme gift. He makes us the repository of the nature and person of the Lord Jesus. "Christ in you, the hope of glory." (Col. 1:19-29.) 10

JESUS CHRIST IS LORD

Jesus Christ has today almost no authority at all among the groups that call themselves by His name.

Among the gospel churches Christ is now in fact little more than a beloved symbol. "All Hail the Power of Jesus' Name" is the church's national anthem and the cross is her official flag, but in the week-by-week services of the church and the day-by-day conduct of her members someone else, not Christ, makes the decisions.

In the conduct of our public worship where is the authority of Christ to be found? The truth is that today the Lord rarely controls a service, and the influence He exerts is very small. We sing of Him and preach about Him, but He must not interfere; we worship our way, and it must be right because we have always done it that way.

For the true Christian the one supreme test for the present soundness and ultimate worth of everything religious must be the place our Lord occupies in it. Is He Lord or symbol? Is He in charge of the project or merely one of the crew?

Does He decide things or only help to carry out the plans of others? All religious activities may be proved by the answer to the question, Is Jesus Christ Lord in this act?   21

There are a great many bogus Christs among us these days. John Owen, the old Puritan, warned people in his day: "You have an imaginary Christ and if you are satisfied with an imaginary Christ you must be satisfied with imaginary salvation."

There is only one Christ and the truly saved man has an attachment to Christ that is intellectual in that he knows who Christ is theologically. For you know there is the romantic Christ of the female novelist and there is the sentimental Christ of the half-converted cowboy and there is the philosophical Christ of the academic egghead and there is the cosy Christ of the effeminate poet and there is the muscular Christ of the all-American halfback. But there is only one true Christ, and God has said that He is His Son.   14

We are under constant temptation these days to substitute another Christ for the Christ of the New Testament.

Even among those who acknowledge the diety of Christ there is often a failure to recognize His manhood. We are quick to assert that when He walked the earth He was *God with men*, but we overlook a truth equally as important, that where He sits now on His mediatorial throne He is *Man with God*. The teaching of the New Testament is that now, at this very moment, there is a man in heaven appearing in the presence of God for us. He is as certainly a man as was Adam or Moses or Paul. He is a man glorified, but His glorification did not dehumanize Him. Today He is a real man, of the race of mankind.

Salvation comes not by "accepting the finished work" or "deciding for Christ." It comes by believing on the Lord Jesus Christ, the whole, living, victorious Lord Who as God and man, fought our fight and won it, accepted our debt as His own and paid it, took our sins and died under them and rose again to set us free. This is the true Christ, and nothing less will do.

But something less is among us, nevertheless, and we do well to identify it so that we may repudiate it. That something is a poetic fiction, a product of the romantic imagination and maudlin religious fancy. It is a Jesus, gentle, dreamy, shy, sweet, almost effeminate, and marvellously adaptable to whatever society He may find Himself in. He is used as a means to almost any carnal end, but He is never acknowledged as Lord. These quasi Christians follow a quasi Christ. They want His help but not His interference. They will flatter Him but never obey Him.

The argument of the apostles is that the Man Jesus has been made higher than angels, higher than Moses and Aaron, higher than any creature in earth or heaven. And this exalted position He attained *as a man*. As God He already stood infinitely above all other beings. The apostles were not declaring the preeminence of God, which would have been superfluous, but of a man, which was necessary.

Those first Christians believed that Jesus of Nazareth, a man they knew, had been raised to a position of Lordship over the universe. He was still their friend, still one of them, but had left them for a while to appear in the presence of God on their behalf. And the proof of this was the presence of the Holy Spirit among them.

One cause of our moral weakness today is an inadequate Christology. We think of Christ as God but fail to conceive of Him as a man glorified. To recapture the power of the early Church we must believe what they believed. And they believed they had a God-approved man representing them in heaven. 4

Let us look out calmly upon the world; or better yet, let us look down upon it from above where Christ is seated and we are seated in Him. 4

The discredited doctrine of a divided Christ goes like this: "Christ is both Savior and Lord. A sinner may be saved by accepting Him as Savior without yielding to Him as Lord." Christ's saviorhood is forever united to His lordship. Christ must be Lord or He will not be Savior. 7

To teach that Christ will use His sacred power to further our worldly interests is to wrong our Lord and injure our own souls. We modern evangelicals need to learn the truths of the sovereignty of God and the lordship of Christ. God will not play along with Adam; Christ will not be used by any of Adam's selfish brood. We had better learn these things fast if this generation of young Christians is to be spared the supreme tragedy of following a Christ who is merely a Christ of convenience and not the true Lord of glory after all. 7

The Spirit never bears witness to an argument about Christ, but He never fails to witness to a proclamation of Christ crucified, dead and buried, and now ascended to the right hand of the Majesty on high. 1

Jesus Christ has today almost no authority at all among the groups that call themselves by His name.

The present position of Christ in the gospel churches may be likened to that of a king in a limited, constitutional monarchy. The king is in such a country no more than a traditional rallying point, a pleasant symbol of unity and loyalty much like a flag or a national anthem. He is lauded, feted and supported, but his real authority is small. Nominally he is head over all, but in every crisis someone else makes the decisions. 21

THE HOLY SPIRIT IS INDISPENSABLE

In my sober judgment the relation of the Spirit to the believer is the most vital question the church faces today.   12

Satan has opposed the doctrine of the Spirit-filled life about as bitterly as any other doctrine there is. He has confused it, opposed it, surrounded it with false notions and fears. He has blocked every effort of the Church of Christ to receive from the Father her divine and blood-bought patrimony. The Church has tragically neglected this great liberating truth—that there is now for the child of God a full and wonderful and completely satisfying anointing with the Holy Ghost.

The Spirit-filled life is not a special, deluxe edition of Christianity. It is part and parcel of the total plan of God for His people. There is nothing about the Holy Spirit queer or strange or eerie.

Unless you are convinced that it isn't an added, unusual, extra, deluxe something that you have to go to God and beg and beat your fists on the chair to get, I recommend that you don't do anything about it yet except to meditate upon the Scriptures bearing on this truth. You don't have to persuade God at all. Dr. Simpson used to say, "Being filled with the Spirit is as easy as breathing; you can simply breathe out and breathe in."

Before you can be filled with the Spirit you must desire to be filled. Are you sure that you want to be possessed by a Spirit other than your own? That Spirit, if He ever possesses you, will be the Lord of your Life! Do you want to hand the keys of your soul over to the Holy Spirit?

Again, are you sure that you need to be filled? Can't you get along the way you are? But maybe you feel in your heart that you just can't go on as you are. If you feel that there are levels of spirituality, mystic deeps and heights of spiritual communion, purity and power that you have never known, that there is fruit which you know you should bear and do not, victory which you know you should have and have not—I would say, "Come on," because God has something for you.

Here is how to receive. First, present your body to Him (Rom. 12:1-2). God can't fill what He can't have. Now I ask you: Are you ready to present your body with all of its functions and all that it contains—your mind, your personality, your spirit, your love, your ambitions, your all? The second thing is to *ask* (Luke 11:9-11), and I set aside all theological objections to this text. He chooses to have us ask; so why not ask? Acts 5:32 tells us the third thing. God gives His Holy Spirit to them that obey Him. Simply live by the Scriptures as you understand them. Simple, but revolutionary. The next thing is, have faith. (Gal. 3:2) We receive Him by faith as we receive the Lord in salvation by faith. He comes as a gift of God to us in power. First He comes in some degree and measure when we are converted, otherwise we couldn't be converted. But I am talking about something different now, an advance over that. I am talking about His coming and possessing the full body and mind and life and heart, taking the whole personality over, gently but directly and bluntly, making it His, so that we may become a habitation of God through the Spirit. 11

When the Spirit presents Christ to our inner vision it has an exhilarating effect on the soul much as wine has on the body. The Spirit-filled man may literally dwell in a state of spiritual fervor amounting to a mild and pure inebriation. God dwells in a state of perpetual enthusiasm. He pursues His labors always in a fulness of holy zeal. 5

The Holy Spirit came to carry the evidence of Christianity from the books of apologetics into the human heart. The Spirit of the living God brought an evidence that needed no logic; it went straight to the soul like a flash of silver light. 11

One blessed treasure we have missed is the right to possess the gifts of the Spirit as set forth in such fulness and clarity in the New Testament.

In their attitude toward the gifts of the Spirit Christians over the last few years have tended to divide themselves into three groups: those who magnify the gifts of the Spirit until they can see little else—those who deny that the gifts of the Spirit are intended for the Church in this period of her history—those who appear to be thoroughly bored with the whole thing and do not care to discuss it.

More recently we have become aware of another group—those who want to know the truth about the Spirit's gifts and to experience whatever God has for them within the context of sound New Testament faith.

It is usually said that there are nine gifts of the Spirit. (I suppose because Paul lists nine in 1 Cor. 12.) Actually Paul mentions no less than seventeen (1 Cor. 12:4-11, 27-31; Rom. 12:3-8; Eph. 4:7-11). And these are not natural talents merely, but gifts imparted by the Holy Spirit to fit the believer for his place in the body of Christ. They are spiritual gifts.

For a generation certain evangelical teachers have told us that the gifts of the Spirit ceased at the death of the apostles or at the completion of the New Testament. This, of course, is a doctrine without a syllable of Biblical authority back of it. The result of this erroneous teaching is that spiritually gifted persons are ominously few among us. This frightening hour calls aloud for men with the gift of prophetic insight. Instead we have men who conduct surveys, polls and panel discussions. We need men with the gift of knowledge. In their place we have men with scholarship—nothing more. Thus, we may be preparing ourselves for the tragic hour when God may set us aside as so-called evangelicals and raise up another movement to keep New Testament Christianity alive in the earth.

The truth of the matter is that the Scriptures plainly imply the imperative of possessing the gifts of the Spirit. But I must also add a word of caution. The various spiritual gifts are not equally valuable, as Paul so carefully explains. Certain brethren have magnified one gift out of seventeen out of all proportion. Among these brethren there have been and are many godly souls, but the general moral results of this teaching have nevertheless not been good. In practice it has resulted in much shameless exhibitionism, a tendency to depend upon experiences instead of upon Christ and often a lack of ability to distinguish the works of the flesh from the operations of the Spirit. Those who deny that the gifts are for us today and those who insist upon making a hobby of one gift are both wrong, and we are all suffering the consequences of their error. 12

The primary work of the Holy Spirit is to restore the lost soul to intimate fellowship with God through the washing of regeneration. Gifts and power for service the Spirit surely desires to impart, but holiness and spiritual worship come first. 8

One obstacle to the reception of power is a widespread fear of our emotions wherever they touch the religious life. Feeling and faith are opposed to each other in modern teaching. This anti-emotionalism is nevertheless an unwarranted inference, not a Scriptural doctrine. Where in the Bible are feeling and faith said to be at odds? The fact is that *faith engenders feeling as certainly as life engenders motion.* Faith as a cold, unemotional light is wholly unknown in the Scriptures. The Book of Acts is almost hilarious with joy.

Another hindrance is fear of fanaticism. Instinctive revulsion from fleshly excesses and foolish undisciplined conduct on the part of some who profess lofty spiritual attainments has closed the door to a life of power for many of God's true children. They have made the mistake of putting all teaching concerning the Holy Spirit in the same category. Such victims must be taught that the Holy Spirit is the Spirit of Jesus, and is as gracious and beautiful as the Saviour Himself. The Holy Spirit is the *cure* for fanaticism, not the cause of it.   13

The doctrine of the Spirit as it relates to the believer has over the last half-century been shrouded in a mist such as lies upon a mountain in stormy weather. A world of confusion has surrounded this truth. This confusion has not come by accident. An enemy has done this. Satan knows that Spiritless evangelicalism is as deadly as Modernism or heresy, and he has done everything in his power to prevent us from enjoying our true Christian heritage.   12

BIBLE TAUGHT *AND* SPIRIT TAUGHT

I believe it was Dr. G. Campbell Morgan who said that the whole truth does not lie in "It is written," but in "It is written" and "Again it is written." The second text must be placed over against the first to balance it and give it symmetry, just as the right wing must work with the left to balance the bird and enable it to fly. Many of the doctrinal divisions among the churches are the result of a blind and stubborn insistence that truth has but one wing. Truth has two wings. 8

For a long time I have believed that truth, to be understood, must be lived; that Bible doctrine is wholly ineffective until it has been digested and assimilated by the total life. The essence of my belief is that there is a difference, a vast difference, between fact and truth. Truth in the Scriptures is more than a fact. A fact may be detached, impersonal, cold and totally disassociated from life. Truth on the other hand, is warm, living and spiritual. A theological fact may be held in the mind for a lifetime without its having any positive effect upon the moral character; but truth is creative, saving, transforming, and it always changes the one who receives it into a humbler and holier man. At what point, then, does a theological fact become for the one that holds it a life-giving truth? *At that point where obedience begins.*

Theological facts are like the altar of Elijah on Carmel before the fire came, correct, properly laid out, but altogether cold. When the heart makes the ultimate surrender, the fire falls and true facts are transmuted into spiritual truth that transforms, enlightens, sanctifies. The church or the individual that is Bible taught without being Spirit taught has simply failed to see that truth lies deeper than the theological statement of it. We only possess what we experience. 8

The devil is a better theologian than any of us and is a devil still. 4

Divine truth is of the nature of spirit and for that reason can be received only by spiritual revelation. God's thoughts belong to the world of spirit, man's to the world of intellect, and while spirit can embrace intellect, the human intellect can never comprehend spirit. Man's thoughts cannot cross over into God's.

God made man in His own image and placed within him an organ by means of which he could know spiritual things. When man sinned that organ—the organ of God-knowledge within the human soul—died. Man by reason cannot know God; he can only *know about* God. When the Spirit illuminates the heart, then a part of the man sees which never saw before; a part of him knows which never knew before, and that with a kind of knowing which the most acute thinker cannot imitate. Man's reason is a fine instrument and useful within its field. It was not given as an organ by which to know God.

Fundamentalism has fallen into the error of textualism, which is simply orthodoxy without the Holy Ghost. Everywhere among conservatives we find persons who are Bible-taught but not Spirit-taught. For a man to understand revealed truth requires an act of God equal to the original act which inspired the text. There is such a thing as a gift of knowing, a gift that comes from heaven. The textualism of our times is based upon the same premise as the old-line rationalism, *confidence in the ability of the human mind to do that which the Bible declares it was never created to do and consequently is wholly incapable of doing.*

The inward kernel of truth has the same configuration as the outward shell. The mind can grasp the shell, but only the Spirit of God can lay hold of the internal essence. Our great error has been that we have trusted to the shell, and have believed we were sound in the faith because we were able to explain the external shape of truth as found in the letter of the Word. From this mortal error Fundamentalism is slowly dying. We have forgotten that the essence of spiritual truth cannot come to the one who knows the external shell of truth unless there is first a miraculous operation of the Spirit within the heart. Those overtones of religious delight that accompany truth when the Spirit illuminates it are all but missing from the Church today. We need to learn that truth consists not in correct doctrine, but in correct doctrine plus the *inward enlightenment of the Holy Spirit.*   2

Reflection upon revealed truth naturally follows the advent of faith, but faith comes first to the hearing ear, not to the cogitating mind.   3

To find the way we need more than light; we need also sight. The Holy Scriptures are the source of moral and spiritual light. Yet I consider that I cast no aspersion upon the hallowed page when I say that its radiance is not by itself enough. Light alone is not sufficient.

Light is a figure which the Bible and religious teachers often use when they mean knowledge. The coming of knowledge is like the rising of the sun. But sunrise means nothing to the unseeing eye. Between light and sight there is a wide difference. One man may have light without sight; he is blind. Another may have sight without light; he is temporarily blind.

What does all this say to us? Simply that religious instruction, however sound, is not enough by itself. It brings light, but it cannot impart sight. The assumption that light and sight are synonymous has brought spiritual tragedy to millions. The Pharisees looked straight at the Light of the World for three years, but not one ray of light reached their inner beings. Light is not enough. The inward operation of the Holy Spirit is necessary to saving faith. The gospel is light but only the Spirit can give sight.   1

While we all pride ourselves that we draw our beliefs from the Holy Scriptures, along those border lines where good men disagree we may unconsciously take sides with our temperament. Cast of mind may easily determine our views when the Scriptures are not clear.   4

Probably no other portion of the Scriptures can compare with the Pauline epistles when it comes to making artificial saints. Peter warned that the unlearned and the unstable would wrest Paul's writings to their own destruction. The ominous thing is that the Pauline doctrines may be taught with complete faithfulness to the letter of the text without making the hearers one whit the better. 5

Significant, isn't it, that of all who hold the evangelical position, those Christians who lay the greatest store by Paul, are often the least Pauline in spirit. There is a vast and important difference between a Pauline creed and a Pauline life. Tens of thousands of believers who pride themselves on their understanding of Romans and Ephesians cannot conceal the sharp spiritual contradiction that exists between their hearts and the heart of Paul.

Paul was a seeker and a finder and a seeker still. They seek and find and seek no more. For them the truth becomes a veil to hide the face of God; for Paul it was a door into His very Presence. Paul's spirit was that of the loving explorer. He was a prospector among the hills of God searching for the gold of personal spiritual acquaintance. Many today stand by Paul's doctrine who will not follow him in his passionate yearning for divine reality. 12

'Truth that is not experienced is no better than error, and may be fully as dangerous. The scribes who sat in Moses' seat were not the victims of error; they were the victims of their failure to experience the truth they taught. 7

THE OLD CROSS
AND THE NEW

All unannounced, and mostly undetected, there has come in modern times a new cross into popular evangelical circles.

From this new cross has sprung a new philosophy of the Christian life, and from that new philosophy has come a new evangelical technique—a new type of meeting and a new kind of preaching.

The old cross would have no truck with the world. For Adam's proud flesh it meant the end of the journey. The new cross, if understood aright, is the source of oceans of good clean fun and innocent enjoyment. It lets Adam live without interference. His life motivation is unchanged; he still lives for his own pleasure.

The new cross does not slay the sinner, it redirects him. It gears him into a cleaner and jollier way of living and saves his self-respect.

The old cross is a symbol of death. God salvages the individual by liquidating him and then raising him again to newness of life. God offers life, but not an improved old life. The life He offers is life out of death. It stands always on the far side of the cross.   20

Among the plastic saints of our times Jesus has to do all the dying and all we want is to hear another sermon about His dying.   17

We want to be saved but we insist that Christ do all the dying. No cross for us, no dethronement, no dying. We remain king within the little kingdom of Mansoul and wear our tinsel crown with all the pride of a Caesar; but we doom ourselves to shadows and weakness and spiritual sterility.   7

So subtle is self that scarcely anyone is conscious of its presence. Because man is born a rebel, he is unaware that he is one. His constant assertion of self, as far as he thinks of it all, appears to him a perfectly normal thing. He is willing to share himself, sometimes even to sacrifice himself for a desired end, but never to dethrone himself.

Sin has many manifestations but its essence is one. A moral being, created to worship before the throne of God, sits on the throne of his own selfhood and from that elevated position declares, "I AM." That is sin in its concentrated essence; yet because it is natural it appears to be good. "What shall we do?" (Acts 2:37) is the deep heart cry of every man who suddenly realizes that he is a usurper and sits on a stolen throne.   3

Promoting self under the guise of promoting Christ is currently so common as to excite little notice. Self can live unrebuked at the very altar. It can watch the bleeding Victim die and not be in the least affected by what it sees. It can fight for the faith of the Reformers and preach elegantly the creed of salvation by faith, and gain strength by its efforts. To tell all the truth, it seems actually to feed upon orthodoxy and is more at home in a Bible Conference than in a tavern. Our very longing after God may afford it an excellent condition under which to thrive and grow.

Self is the opaque veil that hides the Face of God from us. It can be removed only in spiritual experience, never by mere instruction. As well try to instruct leprosy out of our system. There must be a work of God in destruction before we are free. We must invite the cross to do its deadly work within us. We must bring our self-sins to the cross of judgment. 6

Our uncrucified flesh will rob us of purity of heart, Christ-likeness of character, spiritual insight, fruitfulness; and more than all, it will hide from us the vision of God's face, that vision which has been the light of earth and will be the completeness of heaven. 7

Why do we build our churches upon human flesh? For we teach men not to die with Christ but to live in the strength of their dying manhood. 2

One time a young man came to an old saint who taught the deeper life, the crucified life, and said to him, "Father, what does it mean to be crucified?" The old man thought for a moment and said, "Well, to be crucified means three things. First, the man who is crucified is facing only one direction." I like that—facing only one direction. If he hears anything behind him he can't turn around to see what's going on. He has stopped looking back. The crucified man on the cross is looking in only one direction and that is the direction of God and Christ and the Holy Ghost, the direction of Biblical revelation, world evangelization, the edifying of the church, sanctification, and the Spirit-filled life.

And the old man scratched his scraggy grey hair and said, "One thing more, son, about a man on a cross—he's not going back." When you go out to die on the cross you bid good-bye—you are not going back! If we would preach more of this and stop trying to make the Christian life so easy it's contemptible we would have more converts that would last. Get a man converted who knows that if he joins Jesus Christ he's finished, and that while he's going to come up and live anew, as far as this world's concerned he is not going back—then you have a real Christian indeed.

The old man went on, "Another thing about the man on the cross, son; he has no further plans of his own." I like that. Somebody else made his plans for him, and when they nailed him up there all his plans disappeared. Oh, what busy-beaver Christians we are with all of our plans!

It is beautiful to say "I am crucified with Christ," and know that Christ is making your plans. 14

The man who takes his cross and follows Christ will soon find that his direction is *away* from the sepulchre. Death is behind him and a joyous and increasing life before. 2

If I see aright, the cross of popular evangelicalism is not the cross of the New Testament. It is, rather, a new bright ornament upon the bosom of a self-assured and carnal Christianity. The old cross slew men; the new cross entertains them. The old cross condemned; the new cross amuses. The old cross destroyed confidence in the flesh; the new cross encourages it. 2

44

CONTRAST NEW TESTAMENT CHRISTIANITY WITH CHRISTIANITY TODAY

The (Early) Church was not an organization merely, not a movement, but a walking incarnation of spiritual energy. The Church began in power, moved in power and moved just as long as she had power. When she no longer had power she dug in for safety and sought to conserve her gains. But her blessings were like the manna: when they tried to keep it overnight it bred worms and stank. So we have had monasticism, scholasticism, institutionalism; and they have all been indicative of the same thing: absence of spiritual power. In Church history every return to New Testament power has marked a new advance somewhere, and every diminution of power has seen the rise of some new mechanism for conservation and defence. If this analysis is reasonably correct, then we are today in a state of very low spiritual energy. 13

The only power God recognizes in His Church is the power of His Spirit; whereas the only power actually recognized today by the majority of evangelicals is the power of man. God does His work by the operation of the Spirit, while Christian leaders attempt to do theirs by the power of trained and devoted intellect. Bright personality has taken the place of the divine afflatus.

Only what is done through the Eternal Spirit will abide eternally. 18

The essence of true religion is spontaneity, the sovereign movings of the Holy Spirit upon and in the free spirit of redeemed men. When religion loses its sovereign character and becomes mere form this spontaniety is lost also, and in its place come precedent, propriety, system—and the file-card mentality. Back of the file-card mentality is the belief that spirituality can be organized. 5

For centuries the Church stood solidly against every form of worldly entertainment, recognizing it for what it was—a device for wasting time, a refuge from the disturbing voice of conscience, a scheme to divert attention from moral accountability. But of late she appears to have decided that if she cannot conquer the great god Entertainment she may as well join forces with him and make what use she can of his power. 7

Christianity is so entangled with the world that millions never guess how radically they have missed the New Testament pattern. Compromise is everywhere. The world is whitewashed just enough to pass inspection by blind men posing as believers. 2

Evangelical Christianity is now tragically below the New Testament standard. Worldliness is an accepted part of our way of life. Our religious mood is social instead of spiritual. We have lost the art of worship. We are not producing saints.

Our models are successful business men, celebrated athletes and theatrical personalities. We carry on our religious activities after the methods of the modern advertiser. Our homes have been turned into theaters. Our literature is shallow and our hymnody borders on sacrilege. And scarcely anyone appears to care. 5

Much that passes for New Testament Christianity is little more than objective truth sweetened with song and made palatable by religious entertainment. 5

Christ calls men to carry a cross; we call them to have fun in His name. He calls them to forsake the world; we assure them that if they but accept Jesus the world is their oyster. He calls them to suffer; we call them to enjoy all the bourgeois comforts modern civilization affords. He calls them to self-abnegation and death; we call them to spread themselves like green bay trees or perchance even to become stars in a pitiful fifth-rate religious zodiac. He calls them to holiness; we call them to a cheap and tawdry happiness that would have been rejected with scorn by the least of the Stoic philosophers. 1

A new Decalogue has been adopted by the neo-Christians of our day, the first word of which reads "Thou shalt not disagree;" and a new set of Beatitudes too, which begins "Blessed are they that tolerate everything, for they shall not be made accountable for anything." It is now the accepted thing to talk over religious differences in public with the understanding that no one will try to convert another or point out errors in his belief. Imagine Moses agreeing to take part in a panel discussion with Israel over the golden calf; or

Elijah engaging in a gentlemanly dialogue with the prophets of Baal. Or try to picture our Lord Jesus Christ seeking a meeting of minds with the Pharisees to iron out differences.

The blessing of God is promised to the peacemaker, but the religious negotiator had better watch his step. Darkness and light can never be brought together by talk. Some things are not negotiable. 4

One hundred religious persons knit into a unity by careful organization do not constitute a church any more than eleven dead men make a football team. The first requisite is life, always. 4

The modern vogue of bringing science to the support of Christianity proves not the truth of the Christian faith but the gnawing uncertainty in the hearts of those who must look to science to give respectability to their faith. 5

Science, the sweet talking goddess which but a short time ago smilingly disposed of the Bible as a trustworthy guide and took the world by the hand to lead it into a man-made millennium, has turned out to be a dragon capable of destroying that same world with a flick of her fiery tail. 1

The Bible tells of another world too fine for the instruments of scientific research to discover. By faith we engage that world and make it ours. It is accessible to us through the blood of the everlasting covenant. 5

DANGEROUS
MISCONCEPTIONS—
THE DEVIL'S BOOBY-TRAPS

"Faith," said the early Lutherans, "is a perturbing thing." But something has happened to the doctrine of justification by faith as Luther taught it.

The faith of Paul and Luther was a revolutionizing thing. It upset the whole life of the individual and made him into another person altogether. It laid hold on the life and brought it under obedience to Christ. It had a finality about it. It snapped shut on a man's heart like a trap. It realigned all life's actions and brought them into accord with the will of God.

Faith now means no more than passive moral acquiescence in the Word of God and the cross of Jesus. To exercise it we have only to rest on one knee and nod our heads in agreement with the instructions of a personal worker intent upon saving our soul. Such a faith as this does not perturb people. It comforts them. The face of their ego is washed and their self-confidence is rescued from discouragement.

People must be told that the Christian religion is

not something they can trifle with. The only man who can be sure he has true Bible faith is the one who has put himself in a position where he cannot go back.   7

In the divine scheme of salvation the doctrine of faith is central. Every benefit flowing from the atonement of Christ comes to the individual through the gateway of faith. We dare take nothing for granted concerning it.

For a number of years my heart has been troubled over the doctrine of faith as it is received and taught among evangelical Christians everywhere. My fear is that the modern conception of faith is not the Biblical one. Faith is not the believing of a statement we know to be true. Faith based upon reason is faith of a kind, it is true; *but it is not the character of Bible faith,* for it follows the evidence infallibly and has nothing of a moral or spiritual nature in it. True faith rests upon the character of God and asks no further proof than the moral perfections of the One who cannot lie. It is enough that God has said it.

Faith as the Bible knows it is confidence in God and His Son Jesus Christ; it is the response of the soul to the divine character as revealed in the Scriptures; and even this response is impossible apart from the prior inworking of the Holy Spirit. Faith is a gift of God to a penitent soul and has nothing whatsoever to do with the senses or the data they afford. Faith is a miracle; it is the ability God gives to trust His Son, and anything that does not result in action in accord with the will of God is not faith but something else short of it.

Faith and morals are two sides of the same coin. Indeed the very essence of faith is moral. Any professed faith in Christ as personal Saviour that does not bring the life under plenary obedience to Christ as Lord is inadequate and must betray its victim at the last. The man that believes will obey. God gives faith to the obedient heart only. Where real repentance is, there is obedience. 4

To escape the error of salvation by works we have fallen into the opposite error of salvation without obedience. 13

God will take nine steps toward us, but He will not take the tenth. He will *incline* us to repent, but He cannot do our repenting for us. 8

A whole new generation of Christians has come up believing that it is possible to "accept" Christ without forsaking the world. 4

Exhalation is as necessary to life as inhalation. To accept Christ it is necessary that we reject whatever is contrary to Him. 8

To "Accept Christ" is to know the meaning of the words "as He is, so are we in this world." (1 John 4:17) We accept His friends as our friends, His enemies as our enemies, His ways as our ways, His rejection as our rejection, His cross as our cross, His life as our life and His future as our future. 8

The whole world has been booby-trapped by the devil. One field where harmless-looking but deadly traps appear in great profusion is the field of prayer. I think of one such false notion. It is that God always answers prayer.

It is explained that God always answers prayer, either by saying "Yes," or by saying "No," or by substituting something else for the desired favor. Now, it would be hard to invent a neater trick than this to save face for the petitioner whose requests have been rejected for non-obedience.

When we go to God with a request, there are two conditions we must meet: (1) we must pray in the will of God, and (2) we must be living lives pleasing to God. 16

When we become too glib in prayer we are most surely talking to ourselves. 1

We believe that our Christian faith is a continuous perpetuation of a major miracle, the new birth. It is a vital and unique work of God in human nature. It is not reasoning yourself into a position, but something happening that cannot be explained; for what happens to a Christian can never be explained by a psychologist. In that great and terrible day there will be those white with shock when they find that they depended on a mental assent to Christianity instead of on a miracle of new birth. 19

"Instant Christianity"—the kind found almost everywhere in gospel circles—came in with the machine age and fails to understand the true nature of the Christian life, which is not static but dynamic and expanding. It overlooks the fact that a new Christian is a living organism as certainly as a new baby is, and must have nourishment and exercise to assure normal growth. 8

A Christian is a born-one, an embodiment of growing life, and as such may be retarded, stunted, undernourished or injured very much as any other organism. Favorable conditions will produce a stronger and healthier organism than will adverse conditions. Lack of proper instructions, for instance, will stunt Christian growth. 5

We Christians must look sharp that our

Christianity does not simply refine our sins without removing them. The big danger is that we assume that we have been delivered from our sins when we have in reality only exchanged one kind of sin for another.

We must, for instance, be careful that our repentance is not simply a change of location. Whereas we once sinned in the far country among the swineherds, we are now chumming with religious persons, considerably cleaner and much more respectable in appearance, to be sure, but no nearer to true heart purity than we were before.

Again, pride may by religious influence be refined to a quiet self-esteem, skillfully dissembled by a neat use of Bible words to disguise a deep selflove which is to God a hateful and intolerable thing. The real trouble is thus not cleared up, but only driven underground.

The gossip and trouble-maker sometimes at conversion turns into a "spiritual counsellor," but often a closer look will reveal the same restless, inquisitive spirit at work. She is still running the same stand, only on the other side of the street. This is Satan's most successful way of getting into the church to cause weakness, backsliding and division.

Many a business transaction which among worldly men we would brand as sharp practice, when carried on by a Christian after he has prayed over it is hailed as a remarkable answer to prayer and a proof that God is a "partner" in the affair.

These are illustrations only, intended to show how sin may alter its appearance without changing its nature. The will of God is that sin should be removed, not merely refined.　1

Real faith invariably produces holiness of heart and righteousness of life.　4

Without faith it is impossible to please God, but not all faith pleases God.

I do not recall another period when faith was as popular as it is today. Faith has come back into favor with almost everybody. The scientist, the cab driver, the philosopher, the actress, the politician, the prize fighter, the housewife—all are ready to recommend faith as the panacea for all our ills, moral, spiritual and economic. If we only believe hard enough we'll make it somehow. So goes the popular chant. What you believe is not important. Only believe.

Back of this is the nebulous idea that faith is an almighty power flowing through the universe which anyone may plug into at will. When it comes in, out go pessimism, fear, defeat and failure; in come optimism, confidence, personal mastery, and unfailing success in war, love, sports, business and politics.

What is overlooked in all this is that faith is good only when it engages truth; when it is made to rest upon falsehood it can and often does lead to eternal tragedy. For it is not enough that we believe; we must believe the right thing about the right One.

True faith requires that we believe everything God has said about Himself, but also that we believe everything He has said about *us*. Until we believe that we are as bad as God says we are, we can never believe that He will do for us what He says He will do. Right here is where popular religion breaks down.

To believe savingly in Jesus Christ is to believe all He has said about Himself and all that the prophets and apostles have said about Him. Let us beware that the Jesus we "accept" is not one we have created out of the dust of our imagination and formed after our own likeness.

True faith commits us to obedience. That dreamy, sentimental faith which ignores the judgments of God against us and listens to the affirmations of the soul is as deadly as cyanide.

Faith in faith is faith astray. To hope for heaven by means of such faith is to drive in the dark across a deep chasm on a bridge that does not quite reach the other side.   5

ERROR AND TRUTH
TRAVEL THE SAME
HIGHWAYS

There are areas of Christian thought, and because of thought then also of life, where likenesses and differences are so difficult to distinguish that we are often hard put to it to escape complete deception. So skilled is error at imitating truth that the two are constantly being mistaken for each other.

It is therefore critically important that the Christian take full advantage of every provision God has made to save him from delusion. These are *prayer, faith, constant meditation on the Scriptures, obedience, humility, hard, serious thought and the illumination of the Holy Spirit.* 8

These are the times that try men's souls. The latter times are upon us and we cannot escape them; we must triumph in the midst of them. (1 Tim. 4:1-2.)

Strange as it may seem, the danger today is greater for the fervent Christian than for the lukewarm and the self-satisfied. The seeker after God's best things is eager to hear anyone who offers a way by which he can obtain them, particularly if it is presented by someone with an attractive personality and a reputation for superior godliness.

Now our Lord Jesus, that great Shepherd of the sheep, has not left His flock to the mercy of the wolves. He has given us the Scriptures, the Holy Spirit and natural powers of observation. "Prove all things; hold fast that which is good," said Paul (1 Thess. 5:21). "Beloved, believe not every spirit. . ." wrote John (1 John 4:1). "Beware of false prophets. . .Ye shall know them by their fruits," our Lord warned (Matt. 7:15-16).

For those who want a rule by which they can test everything I make available here a little secret by which I have tested my own spiritual experiences and religious impulses for many years.

Briefly stated the test is this: This new doctrine, this new religious habit, this new view of truth, this new spiritual experience—*how has it affected my attitude toward and my relation to God, Christ, the Holy Scriptures, self, other Christians, the world and sin.* By this sevenfold test we may prove everything religious.

1. One vital test of all religious experience is how it affects our relation to God, our concept of God and our attitude toward Him. Any doctrine, any experience that serves to magnify Him is likely to be inspired by Him.

The heart of man is like a musical instrument and may be played upon by the Holy Spirit, by an evil spirit or by the spirit of man himself. Religious emotions are very much the same, no matter who the player may be. Many enjoyable feelings may be aroused within the soul by low or even idolatrous worship. The nun who kneels "breathless with adoration" before an image of the Virgin is having a genuine religious experience. She feels love, awe and reverence, all enjoyable emotions, as certainly as if she were adoring God. The mystical experiences of Hindus and Sufis cannot be brushed aside as mere pretense. Neither dare we dismiss the high religious flights of spiritists and other occultists as imagination. These may have and sometimes do have genuine encounters with something or someone beyond themselves. In the same manner Christians are sometimes led into emotional experiences that are beyond their power to comprehend. I have met such and they have inquired eagerly whether or not their experience was of God.

The big test is, What has this done to my relationship to the God and Father of our Lord Jesus Christ? (Rev. 4:11.)

2. The next test is, How has this new experience affected my attitude toward the Lord Jesus Christ? Whatever place present-day religion may give to Christ, God gives Him top place in earth and in heaven. He must stand at the center of all true doctrine, all acceptable practice and all genuine Christian experience. Christless Christianity sounds contradictory but it exists as a real phenomenon in our day.

Again, there are psychic experiences that thrill the seeker and lead him to believe that he has indeed met the Lord and been carried to the third heaven; but the true nature of the phenomenon is discovered later when the face of Christ begins to fade from the victim's consciousness.

If on the other hand the new experience tends to make Christ indispensable, if it takes our interest off our feelings and places it in Christ, we are on the right track. Whatever makes Christ dear to us is pretty sure to be from God. (Matt. 3:17, Acts 2:36, 4:12, John 14:6.)

3. Another revealing test is, How does it affect my attitude toward the Holy Scriptures? Did this new experience, this new view of truth, spring out of the Word of God itself? Whatever originates outside the Scriptures should for that very reason be suspect until it can be shown to be in accord with them. However high the emotional content, no experience can be proved to be genuine unless we can find chapter and verse authority for it in the Scriptures. (Isaiah 8:20.)

Whatever is new or singular should also be viewed with a lot of caution. Over the last half-century quite a number of unscriptural notions have gained acceptance among Christians by claiming that they were among the truths that were to be revealed in the last days. The truth is that the Bible does not teach that there will be new light and advanced spiritual experiences in the latter days; *it teaches the exact opposite.* Beware of any man who claims to be wiser than the apostles or holier than the martyrs of the Early Church.

While true power lies not in the letter of the text but in the Spirit that inspired it, we should never underestimate the value of the letter. The text of truth has the same relation to truth as the honeycomb has to honey. One serves as a receptacle for the other. But there the analogy ends. The honey can be removed from the comb, but the Spirit of truth cannot and does not operate apart from the letter of the Holy Scriptures. For this reason a growing acquaintance with the Holy Spirit will always mean an increasing love for the Bible.

4.   Again, we can prove the quality of religious experience by its effect on self-life. The Holy Spirit and the fallen human self are diametrically opposed to each other. (Gal. 5:17.) Before the Spirit of God can work creatively in our hearts He must have our full consent to displace our natural self with the Person of Christ. This displacement is carefully explained in Romans 6, 7, and 8.

A good rule is this: If this experience has served to humble me and make me little and vile in my own eyes, it is of God, but if it has given me a feeling of self-satisfaction it is false and should be dismissed as emanating from self or the devil. Nothing that comes from God will minister to my pride or self-congratulation.

5.   Our relation to and our attitude toward our fellow Christians is another accurate test. Sometimes an earnest Christian will, after some remarkable spiritual encounter, withdraw himself from his fellow-believers and develop a spirit of faultfinding. He may be honestly convinced that he is now in an advanced state of grace, and that the *hoi polloi* in the church where he attends are but a mixed multitude. This is a dangerous state of mind, and the more dangerous because it can justify itself by the facts. The brother *has* had a remarkable experience. It is not that he is mistaken in his facts that proves him to be in error, but that his reaction to the facts is of the flesh. His new spirituality has made him less

61

charitable. Any religious experience that fails to deepen our love for our fellow Christians may safely be written off as spurious. (1 John 3:18-19, 4:7-8, 5:1, John 13:35.)

6. Another certain test is this: Note how it affects our relation to and our attitude toward "the world." I do not mean, of course, the beautiful order of nature. Neither do I mean the world of lost men. (John 3:16.) Certainly any true touch of God in the soul will deepen our appreciation of nature and intensify our love for the lost. I refer here to the world of carnal enjoyments, of godless pleasures, of the pursuit of earthly riches and reputation and sinful happiness—in short, unregenerate human society romping on its way to hell, the exact opposite of the true Church of God. (1 John 2:15-17, 2 Cor. 6:14.) Any spirit that permits compromise with the world is a false spirit. Any religious movement that imitates the world in any of its manifestations is false to the cross of Christ and on the side of the devil.

7. The last test of the genuineness of Christian experience is what it does to our attitude toward sin. Whatever makes holiness more attractive and sin more intolerable may be accepted as genuine. (Tit. 2:11-13.)

Jesus warned, "There shall arise false Christs, and false prophets, and shall shew great signs and wonders; insomuch that, if it were possible, they should deceive the very elect." (Matt. 24:24.) These words describe our day too well to be coincidental. 4

The farther we push into the sanctuary the greater becomes the danger of self-deception. The deeply religious man is far more vulnerable than the easy-going fellow who takes his religion lightly. This latter may be deceived but he is not likely to be self-deceived. 4

Most men, indeed, play at religion as they play at games, religion itself being of all games the one most universally played. 2

The unattended garden will soon be overrun with weeds; the heart that fails to cultivate truth and root out error will shortly be a theological wilderness. 4

A bit of healthy disbelief is sometimes as needful as faith to the welfare of our souls. It is no sin to doubt some things, but it may be fatal to believe everything. Faith never means gullibility. Credulity never honors God. The gullible mentality is like the ostrich that will gulp down anything that looks interesting. I have met Christians with no more discrimination than the ostrich.

The healthy soul, like the healthy blood stream, has its proper proportion of white and red cells. The red corpuscles are like faith: they carry the life-giving oxygen to every part of the body. The white cells are like disbelief: they pounce upon dead and toxic matter and carry it out to the drain. Thus the two kinds of cells working together keep the tissues in good condition. In the healthy heart there must be provision for keeping dead and poisonous matter out of the life stream. This the credulous person never suspects. He is all for faith.

Along with our faith in God must go a healthy disbelief of everything occult and esoteric. Numerology, astrology, spiritism, and everything weird and strange that passes for religion must be rejected. All this is toxic matter and has no place in the life of a true Christian. He has Christ, and He is the way, the truth and the life. 7

SOME KEYS TO
THE DEEPER LIFE

To speak of the "deeper life" is not to speak of anything deeper than simple New Testament religion. The "deeper life" is deeper only because the average Christian life is tragically shallow. 12

Some people object to taking vows, but in the Bible you will find many great men of God directed by covenants, promises, vows and pledges. A carnal man refuses the discipline of such commitments. He says, "I want to be free. It is legalism." There are many religious tramps in the world who will not be bound by anything.

Now there are five vows I have in mind which we do well to make and keep. 1. *Deal thoroughly with sin.* 2. *Never own anything—get rid of the sense of possessing.* 3. *Never defend yourself.* 4. *Never pass anything on about anybody else that will hurt him.* 5. *Never accept any glory.*

Remember that these five vows are not something you write in the back of your Bible and forget. They have got to be written in your own blood. 9

The Word of God well understood and religiously obeyed is the shortest route to spiritual perfection. And we must not select a few favorite passages to the exclusion of others. Nothing less than a whole Bible can make a whole Christian. 5

Make your thoughts a clean sanctuary. To God, our thoughts are things. Our thoughts are the decorations inside the sanctuary where we live. If our thoughts are purified by the blood of Christ, we are living in a clean room no matter if we are wearing overalls covered with grease. Your thoughts pretty much decide the mood and weather and climate inside your heart, and God considers your thoughts as part of you. Thoughts of peace, thoughts of pity, thoughts of mercy, thoughts of kindness, thoughts of charity, thoughts of God, thoughts of the Son of God—these are pure things, good things, and high things. Therefore, if you would cultivate the Spirit's acquaintance, you must get hold of your thoughts and not allow your mind to be a wilderness in which every kind of unclean beast roams and bird flies. You must have a clean heart. 11

There are two kinds of lives: the fallow and the ploughed. Miracles follow the plough. 13

Paul was a better man for his thorn. 5

Why do some persons "find" God in a way that others do not? He has no favorites within His household. The difference lies not with God but with us.

I venture to suggest that the one vital quality which the great saints had in common was *spiritual receptivity*. They differed from the average person in that when they felt the inward longing they *did something about it.* They acquired the lifelong habit of spiritual response.

Receptivity can be present in degrees, depending upon the individual. It may be increased by exercise or destroyed by neglect. It is not a sovereign and irresistible force which comes upon us as a seizure from above. It is a gift of God, indeed, but one which must be recognized and cultivated.

Failure to see this is the cause of a very serious breakdown in modern evangelicalism. We now demand glamor and fast flowing dramatic action. We have been trying to apply machine-age methods to our relations with God. We read our chapter, have our short devotions and rush away, hoping to make up for our deep inward bankruptcy by attending another gospel meeting or. . .

The tragic results of this spirit are all about us. It will require a determined heart and more than a little courage to wrench ourselves loose from the grip of our times and return to Biblical ways. 6

"Christ in you, the hope of glory." I'm not afraid of the devil. The devil can handle me—he's got judo I never heard of. But he can't handle the One to whom I'm joined; he can't handle the One to whom I'm united; he can't handle the One whose nature dwells in my nature. 10

The man who comes to Christ in the loneliness of personal repentance and faith is also born into a family. The church is called the household of God, and it is the ideal place to rear young Christians. Just as a child will not grow up to be a normal adult if forced to live alone, so the Christian who withdraws from the fellowship of other Christians will suffer great soul injury as a result. Such a one can never hope to develop normally.   1

The Lord cannot fully bless a man until He has first conquered him.   2

We Christians must simplify our lives or lose untold treasures on earth and in eternity. Modern civilization is so complex as to make the devotional life all but impossible.

Science, which has provided men with certain material comforts, has robbed them of their souls by surrounding them with a world hostile to their existence. One way the civilized world destroys men is by preventing them from thinking their own thoughts. Our "vastly improved methods of communication" of which the shortsighted boast so loudly now enable a few men in strategic centers to feed into millions of minds alien thought stuff, ready-made and pre-digested. A little effortless assimilation of these borrowed ideas and the average man has done all the thinking he will or can do. This subtle brain-washing goes on day after day.

The need for solitude and quietness was never greater than it is today.   5

To have faith we must immerse ourselves in the Scriptures. And faith must be exercised if it is to be effective. Faith, like a muscle, grows by stretching.   8

Strive to get beyond mere pensive longing. Set your face like a flint and begin to put your life in order. Every man is as holy as he really wants to be. But the want must be all-compelling.

Tie up the loose ends of your life. Begin to tithe. . .institute family prayer. . .pay up your debts. . .make restitution. . .set aside time to pray and search the Scriptures. . .surrender wholly to the will of God.

Put away every un-Chrisitan habit from you. If other Christians practice it without compunction, God may be calling you to come nearer to Him than these care to come. Remember the words, "Others may, you cannot." Do not condemn or criticize, but seek a better way.

Get Christ Himself in the focus of your heart and keep Him there continually. Only in Christ will you find complete fulfillment.

Throw your heart open to the Holy Spirit and invite Him to fill you. He will do it. Let no one interpret the Scriptures for you in such a way as to rule out the Father's gift of the Spirit. Every man is as full of the Spirit as he wants to be. Make your heart a vacuum and the Spirit will rush in to fill it.

Be hard on yourself and easy on others. Carry your own cross but never lay one on the back of another.

Begin to practice the presence of God.   4

SERVING IN
THE EMERGENCY

The fall of man has created a perpetual crisis. It will last until sin has been put down and Christ reigns over a redeemed and restored world. Until that time the earth remains a disaster area and its inhabitants live in a state of extraordinary emergency.

To me it has always been difficult to understand those evangelical Christians who insist upon living in the crisis as if no crisis existed. They say they serve the Lord, but they divide their days so as to leave plenty of time to play and loaf and enjoy the pleasures of the world as well. They are at ease while the world burns. 1

Before the judgment seat of Christ my service will be judged not by how much I have done but by how much I could have done. In God's sight my giving is measured not by how much I have given but by how much I could have given and how much I had left after I made my gift. The needs of the world and my total ability to minister to those needs decide the worth of my service.

Not by its size is my gift judged, but by how

much of me there is in it. No man gives at all until he has given all. No man gives anything acceptable to God until he has first given himself in love and sacrifice. 8

Almighty God, just because He is almighty, needs no support. Twentieth-century Christianity has put God on charity. So lofty is our opinion of ourselves that we find it quite easy, not to say enjoyable, to believe that we are necessary to God.

I fear that thousands of young persons enter Christian service from no higher motive than to help deliver God from the embarrassing situation His love has gotten Him into and His limited abilities seem unable to get Him out of. Add to this a certain degree of commendable idealism and a fair amount of compassion for the under-privileged and you have the true drive behind much Christian activity today.

Let us not imagine that the truth of the divine self-sufficiency will paralyze Christian activity. Rather it will stimulate all holy endeavor. This truth, while a needed rebuke to human self-confidence, will when viewed in its Biblical perspective lift from our minds the exhausting load of mortality and encourage us to take the easy yoke of Christ and spend ourselves in Spirit-inspired toil for the honor of God and the good of mankind. For the blessed news is that the God who needs no one has in sovereign condescension stooped to work by and in and through His obedient children. 3

The faith of Christ offers no buttons to push for quick service. The new order must wait the Lord's own time, and that is too much for the man in a hurry. He just gives up and becomes interested in something else.   4

The task of the church is twofold: to spread Christianity throughout the world and to make sure that the Christianity she spreads is the pure New Testament kind. Christianity will always reproduce itself after its kind. A worldly minded, unspiritual church is sure to bring forth on other shores a Christianity much like her own. Not the naked Word only but the character of the witness determines the quality of the convert.

The popular notion that the first obligation of the church is to spread the gospel to the uttermost parts of the earth is false. *Her first obligation is to be spiritually worthy to spread it.* Our Lord said "Go ye," but He also said "Tarry ye," and the tarrying had to come before the going. Had the disciples gone forth as missionaries before the day of Pentecost it would have been an overwhelming spiritual disaster, for they could have done no more than make converts after their own likeness.

To spread an effete, degenerate brand of Christianity to pagan lands is not to fulfill the commandment of Christ or discharge our obligation to the heathen. Increased numbers of demi-Christians is not enough.   5

It is often difficult to tell in a given instance whether we have been defeated or are victorious in a conflict. Sometimes what looks like a defeat will be seen later to have been a positive victory. And it must not be forgotten that this principle works just the same in reverse.

Our Lord could die with the same calm in which He had lived. He had known all along how things would turn out. He knew His apparent defeat would eventuate in universal glory for the human race.   7

Our Lord died an apparent failure, discredited by the leaders of established religion, rejected by society and forsaken by his friends. It took the resurrection to demonstrate how gloriously Christ had triumphed.

Yet today the professed church seems to have learned nothing. How much eager-beaver religious work is done out of a carnal desire to make good.   1

Compromise will take the pressure off. Satan will not bother a man who has quit fighting. But the cost of quitting will be a life of peaceful stagnation. We sons of eternity just cannot afford such a thing.   8

If only we would stop lamenting and look up. God is here. Christ is risen. The Spirit has been poured out from on high. All this we know as theological truth. It remains for us to turn it into joyous spiritual experience by faith, love and obedience.   8

COUNSEL FOR
FAITH'S JOURNEY

To believe actively that our Heavenly Father constantly spreads around us providential circumstances that work for our present good and our everlasting well-being brings to the soul a veritable benediction. 3

Whatever keeps me from the Bible is my enemy, however harmless it may appear to be. Whatever engages my attention when I should be meditating on God and things eternal does injury to my soul. Let the cares of life crowd out the Scriptures from my mind and I have suffered loss where I can least afford it. Let me accept anything else instead of the Scriptures and I have been cheated and robbed to my eternal confusion. 8

One of the puzzling questions likely to turn up sooner or later to vex the seeking Christian is how he can fulfill the Scriptural command to love God with all his heart and his neighbor as himself. He wants to, but he cannot. The delightful wells of feeling simply will not flow. How can I love by commandment?

To find our way out of the shadows and into the

cheerful sunlight we need only to know that there are two kinds of love: the love of *feeling* and the love of *willing*. The one lies in the emotions, the other in the will. The love the Bible enjoins is not the love of feeling; *it is the love of willing, the willed tendency of the heart.* (For these two happy phrases I am indebted to another.) *Religion lies in the will and so does righteousness.* The will is the automatic pilot that keeps the soul on course. The will, not the feelings, determines moral direction. The root of all evil in human nature is the corruption of the will. The prodigal son took his first step upward from the pigsty when he said, "I will arise and go to my father." As he had once willed to leave his father's house, now he willed to return.

To love God with all our heart we must first of all *will* to do so. We should repent our lack of love and determine from this moment on to make God the object of our devotion. We shall soon find to our great delight that our feelings are beginning to move in the direction of the "willed tendency of the heart." Our emotions will become disciplined and directed. We shall begin to taste the "piercing sweetness" of the love of Christ. The whole life, like a delicate instrument, will be tuned to sing the praises of Him who loved us and washed us from our sins in His own blood. But first of all we must will, for the will is master of the heart.   4

Remember that *sin is not the only cause of dryness.* "Religion," say the theologians, "lies in the will." What our will is set to do is what really matters at last. Feeling is the play of emotion over the will, a kind of musical accompaniment to the business of living, and while it is indeed most enjoyable to have the band play as we march to Zion, it is by no means indispensable. We can work and walk without music and if we have true faith we can walk with God without feeling. 7

No one enjoys walking into a cold wind. Yet the church has had to march with the wind in her face through the long centuries. 8

The widest thing in the universe is not space; it is the potential capacity of the human heart. Being made in the image of God, it is capable of almost unlimited extension in all directions. And one of the world's worst tragedies is that we allow our hearts to shrink until there is room in them for little beside ourselves. Of all persons Christians should have the largest hearts. One of the most stinging criticisms made against Christians is that their minds are narrow and their hearts small. This may not be wholly true, but that such a charge can be made at all is sufficient cause for serious heart searching and prayer. 7

All things else being equal, our prayers are only as powerful as our lives. In the long pull we pray only as well as we live. 7

In this world of corruption there is real danger that the earnest Christian may overreact in his resistance to evil and become a victim of the religious occupational disease, cynicism. The constant need to go counter to popular trends may easily develop in him a sour habit of faultfinding and turn him into a sulky critic of other men's matters, without charity and without love.

What makes this cynical spirit particularly dangerous is that the cynic is usually right. His analyses are accurate, his judgment sound; yet for all that he is wrong, frightfully, pathetically wrong.

As a cure for the sour, faultfinding attitude I recommend the cultivation of the habit of thankfulness. Thanksgiving has great curative powers. A thankful heart cannot be cynical. 7

It requires great care and a true knowledge of ourselves to distinguish a spiritual burden from religious irritation. 4

Often acts done in a spirit of religious irritation have consequences far beyond anything we could have guessed. 5

Always it is more important that we retain a right spirit toward others than that we bring them to our way of thinking, even if our way is right. 5

Satan cares little whether we go astray after a false doctrine or merely turn sour. Either way he wins. 8

One serious and often distressing problem for many Christians is their feeling that God is far from them. It is hard to rejoice in the Lord when we are suffering from this sense of remoteness. It is like trying to have a warm, bright summer without the sun.

Let us reason together about this. In spiritual matters we think correctly only when we boldly rule out the concept of space. God is spirit, and spirit dwells not in space. Space has to do with matter and spirit is independent of it. We should never think of God as being spatially near or remote. God is infinite and in His infinitude He swallows up all space. God is not contained: He contains. (2 Chron. 6:18.)

Yet when we speak of men being "far" from God we speak truly. The Lord said of Israel, "Their heart is far from me," and there we have the definition of far and near in our relation to God. The words refer not to physical distance, but to likeness. It is dissimilarity that creates the sense of remoteness between creatures and between men and God.

For the moral unlikeness between man and God the Bible has a word, alienation. Fallen human nature is precisely opposite to the nature of God as revealed in Jesus Christ. Because there is no moral likeness there is no communion, hence the feeling that God is far away in space. This erroneous notion discourages prayer and prevents many a sinner from believing unto life. The truth is that He is nearer to us than we are to ourselves. (Acts 17:27-28.)

But how can the conscious sinner bridge the mighty gulf that separates him from God in living experience? The answer is that he cannot, but the glory of the Christian message is that Christ did. (Col. 1:21-22.) The new birth makes us partakers of the divine nature. There the work of undoing the dissimilarity between us and God begins. From there it progresses by the sanctifying operation of the Holy Spirit till God is satisfied.

But as I said, even the regenerated soul may sometimes suffer from the feeling that God is far from him. What then should he do? First, the trouble may be no more than a temporary break in God-conscious communion due to any one of half a hundred causes. Trust God in the dark till the light returns. Second, should the sense of remoteness persist in spite of prayer and what you believe is faith, look to your inner life for evidences of wrong attitudes, evil thoughts or dispositional flaws. These are unlike God and create a psychological gulf between you and Him. Put away the evil from you, believe, and the sense of nearness will be restored. God was never away in the first place.   1

It is a splendid rule to refrain from making decisions when we are discouraged .   5

Periods of staleness in the life are not inevitable but they are common. He is a rare Christian who has not experienced times of spiritual dullness. Sometimes our trouble is not moral but physical. The Christian who gets tired in the work of the Lord and stays tired without relief beyond a reasonable time will go stale.

We can keep from going stale by getting proper rest, by practicing complete candor in prayer, by introducing variety into our lives, by heeding God's call to move onward and by exercising quiet faith always.   8

Stop trying to compete with others. Give yourself to God and then be what and who you are without regard to what others think. Reduce your interests to a few. Don't try to know what will be of no service to you. Avoid the digest type of mind. Learn to pray inwardly every moment. Practice candor, childlike honesty, humility. Pray for a single eye. Read less, but read more of what is important to your inner life. Call home your roving thoughts. Gaze on Christ with the eyes of your soul. Practice spiritual concentration.   5

The purest saint at the moment of his greatest strength is as weak as he was before his conversion. What has happened is that he has switched from his little human battery to the infinite power of God. He has quite literally exchanged weakness for strength, but the strength is not his; it flows into him from God as long as he abides in Christ. "They that wait upon the Lord shall *exchange* their strength." (Isaiah 40:31.)   8

OUR NEED TODAY

It is time for us to seek again the leadership of the Holy Ghost. Man's lordship has cost us too much. Man's intrusive will has introduced such a multiplicity of unspiritual ways and unscriptural activities as positively to threaten the life of the Church. 2

We need a baptism of clear seeing. We desperately need seers who can see through the mist—Christian leaders with prophetic vision. Unless they come soon it will be too late for this generation. And if they do come we will no doubt crucify a few of them in the name of our wordly orthodoxy. 7

Between the scribe who has read and the prophet who has seen there is a difference as wide as the sea. We are today overrun with orthodox scribes, but the prophets, where are they? The hard voice of the scribe sounds over evangelicalism, but the Church waits for the tender voice of the saint who has penetrated the veil and has gazed with inward eye upon the Wonder that is God. 6

If the church in the second half of this century is to recover from the injuries she suffered in the first half, there must appear a new type of preacher. The proper, ruler-of-the-synagogue type will never do. Neither will the priestly type of man who carries out his duties, takes his pay and asks no questions, nor the smooth-talking pastoral type who knows how to make the Christian religion acceptable to everyone. All these have been tried and found wanting. Another kind of religious leader must arise among us. He must be of the old prophet type, a man who has seen visions of God and has heard a voice from the Throne. 5

Unless we intend to reform we may as well not pray. To beg for a flood of blessing to come upon a backslidden and disobedient Church is to waste time and effort. We must return to New Testament Christianity, not in creed only but in complete manner of life as well. Separation, obedience, humility, simplicity, gravity, self-control, modesty, cross-bearing: these all must again be made a living part of the total Christian concept and be carried out in everyday conduct. We must cleanse the temple of the hucksters and the money changers and come fully under the authority of our risen Lord once more. 12

Have you noticed how much praying for revival has been going on of late—and how little revival has resulted? I believe our problem is that we have been trying to substitute praying for obeying, and it simply will not work. To pray for revival while ignoring or actually flouting the plain precept laid down in the Scriptures is to waste a lot of words and get nothing for our trouble. Prayer will become effective when we stop using it as a substitute for obedience. 5

The great need of the hour among persons spiritually hungry is twofold: first, to know the Scriptures, apart from which no saving truth will be vouchsafed by our Lord; the second, to be enlightened by the Spirit, apart from Whom the Scriptures will not be understood. 7

The message "Christ in you, the hope of glory," needs to be restored to the Church. We must show a new generation of nervous, almost frantic, Christians that power lies at the center of the life. 7

Dispositional sins are fully as injurious to the Christian cause as the more overt acts of wickedness. Let us list a few of them: sensitiveness, irritability, churlishness, faultfinding, peevishness, temper, resentfulness, cruelty, uncharitable attitudes; and of course there are many more. Many persons who had been secretly longing to find Christ have been turned away and embittered by manifestations of ugly dispositional flaws in the lives of the very persons who were trying to win them. Unsaintly saints are the tragedy of Christianity. 5

I am afraid we modern Christians are long on talk and short on conduct. We use the language of power but our deeds are the deeds of weakness. We settle for words in religion because deeds are too costly. It is easier to pray, "Lord, help me to carry my cross daily" than to pick up the cross and carry it; but since the mere request for help to do something we do not actually intend to do has a certain degree of religious comfort, we are content with repetition of the words. 1

In the Church of God two opposite dangers are

to be recognized and avoided; they are a cold heart and a hot head.

It may be said without qualification that there can never be too much fire, if it is the true fire of God; and it can be said as certainly that there cannot be too much cool judgment in religious matters if that judgment is sanctified by the Spirit. The history of revivals in the Church reveals how harmful the hot head can be.

Among the gifts of the Spirit scarcely any one is of greater practical usefulness than the gift of discernment. This gift should be highly valued and frankly sought as being almost indispensable in these critical times. This gift will enable us to distinguish the chaff from the wheat and to divide the manifestations of the flesh from the operations of the Spirit.

Human sweat can add nothing to the work of the Spirit, especially when it is nerve sweat. The hottest fire of God is cool when it touches the redeemed intellect. It makes the heart glow but leaves the judgment completely calm. These are days of great religious turmoil. Let love burn on with increasing fervor but bring every act to the test of quiet wisdom. Keep the fire in the furnace where it belongs. An overheated chimney will create more excitement than a well controlled furnace, but it is likely to burn the house down. Let the rule be: a hot furnace but a cool chimney. 7

The essence of idolatry is the entertainment of thoughts about God that are unworthy of Him. The heaviest obligation lying upon the Christian Church today is to purify and elevate her concept of God until it is once more worthy of Him—and of her. 3

The world is evil, the times are waxing late, and the glory of God has departed from the church as the fiery cloud once lifted from the door of the Temple in the sight of Ezekiel the prophet.

The God of Abraham has withdrawn His conscious Presence from us, and another God whom our fathers knew not is making himself at home among us. This God we have made and because we have made him we can understand him; because we have created him he can never surprise us , never overwhelm us, nor astonish us, nor transcend us.

The God of glory sometimes revealed Himself like a sun to warm and bless, indeed, but often to astonish, overwhelm, and blind before He healed and bestowed permanent sight. This God of our fathers wills to be the God of their succeeding race. We have only to prepare Him a habitation in love and faith and humility. We have but to want Him badly enough, and He will come and manifest Himself to us.   3

Almost every day of my life I am praying that "a jubilant pining and longing for God" might come back on the evangelical churches. We don't need to have our doctrine straightened out; we are as orthodox as the Pharisees of old. But this longing for God that brings spiritual torrents and whirlwinds of seeking and self-denial—this is almost gone from our midst.   17

A FINAL SELECTION

The blight of the Pharisee's heart in olden times was doctrine without love. We are safe only when the love of God is shed abroad in our hearts by the Holy Ghost, only when our intellects are indwelt by the loving Fire that came at Pentecost. 2

Our Lord told His disciples that love and obedience were organically united. The final test of love is obedience. 8

Faith, as Paul saw it, was a living, flaming thing leading to surrender and obedience to the commandments of Christ. 13

The returning sinner is not saved by some judicial transaction apart from a corresponding moral change. Salvation must include a judicial change of status, but what is overlooked by most teachers is that it *also includes an actual change in the life of the individual.* And by this we mean more than a surface change, we mean a transformation as deep as the roots of his human life. 2

That this world is a playground instead of a battleground has now been accepted in practice by the vast majority of fundamentalist Christians. They are facing both ways, enjoying Christ and the world too.   22

It is scarcely possible in most places to get anyone to attend a meeting where the only attraction is God.   4

Only that is of God which honors the Spirit and prospers at the expense of the human ego.   2

The meek man is not a human mouse afflicted with a sense of his own inferiority. Rather he may be in his moral life as bold as a lion and as strong as Samson, but he has stopped being fooled about himself. He has accepted God's estimate of his own life. He knows he is as weak and helpless as God has declared him to be, but paradoxically, he knows at the same time that he is in the sight of God more important than angels. In himself, nothing; in God, everything. That is his motto.   6

More spiritual progress can be made in one short moment of speechless silence in the awesome presence of God than in years of mere study. It is only when our vaunted wisdom has been met and defeated in a breathless encounter with Omniscience that we are permitted really to know, when prostrate and wordless the soul receives divine knowledge like a flash of light on a sensitized plate. The exposure may be brief, but the results are permanent.   7

That God has placed before His redeemed children a vast world of spiritual treasures and that they refuse or neglect to claim it may easily turn out to be the second greatest tragedy in the history of the moral creation, the first and greatest being the fall of man.   8

For everyone that actually crosses over into the

Promised Land there are many who stand for awhile and look longingly across the river and then turn sadly back to the comparative safety of the sandy wastes of the old life. 1

It may be said without qualification that every man is as holy and as full of the Spirit as he wants to be. He may not be as full as he wishes he were, but he is most certainly as full as he wants to be. 1

Grace will save a man but it will not save him and his idol. 4

If in His absolute freedom God has willed to give man limited freedom, who is there to stay his hand or say, "What doest thou?" Man's will is free because God is sovereign. A God less than sovereign could not bestow moral freedom upon his creatures. He would be afraid to do so. 3

Salvation is from our side a choice; from the divine side it is a seizing upon, an apprehending, a conquest by the Most High God. Our *"accepting"* and *"willing"* are reactions rather than actions. The right of determination must always remain with God. 2

Of all work done under the sun religious work should be the most open to examination. There is positively no place in the church for sleight of hand or double talk. Everything done by the churches should be completely above suspicion. The true church will have nothing to hide. 5

The true church is the repository of the life of God among men, and if in one place the frail vessels fail, that life will break out somewhere else. Of this we may be sure. A local church can die. The Church cannot die. 4

Keep your feet on the ground, but let your heart

soar as high as it will. Refuse to be average or to surrender to the chill of your spiritual environment. 7

As long as we remain in the body we shall be subject to a certain amount of that common suffering which we must share with all the sons of men.

But there is another kind of suffering, known only to the Christian: it is voluntary suffering deliberately and knowingly incurred for the sake of Christ. Such is a luxury, a treasure of fabulous value. And it is rare as well as precious, for there are few in this decadent age who will of their own choice go down into this dark mine looking for jewels. God will not force us into this kind of suffering; He will not lay this cross upon us nor embarrass us with riches we do not want. Such riches are reserved for those who apply to serve in the legion of the expendables, who love not their lives unto the death, who volunteer to suffer for Christ's sake and who follow up their application with lives that challenge the devil and invite the fury of hell. Such as these have said good-bye to the world's toys; they have accepted toil and suffering as their earthly portion. The marks of the cross are upon them and they are known in heaven and in hell. But where are they? Has this breed of Christian died out of the earth? 7

We can afford to suffer now; we'll have a long eternity to enjoy ourselves. 1

In this hour of all-but-universal darkness one cheering gleam appears: within the fold of conservative Christianity there are to be found increasing numbers of persons whose religious lives are marked by a growing hunger after God

Himself. They are eager for spiritual realities and will not be put off with words, nor will they be content with correct "interpretations" of truth. They are athirst for God, and they will not be satisfied till they have drunk deep at the Fountain of Living Water. This is the only real harbinger of revival which I have been able to detect anywhere on the religious horizon.   6

KEY TO EXTRACTS

Books
1. Born After Midnight
2. The Divine Conquest
3. The Knowledge of the Holy
4. Man: The Dwelling Place of God
5. Of God and Men
6. The Pursuit of God
7. The Root of the Righteous
8. That Incredible Christian

Booklets
9. Five Vows for Spiritual Power
10. God's Greatest Gift to Man
11. How to be Filled with the Holy Spirit
12. Keys to the Deeper Life
13. Paths to Power
14. Total Commitment to Christ
15. Worship: The Missing Jewel in the Evangelical Church

Leaflets
16. Does God Always Answer Prayer?
17. Three Faithful Wounds
18. The Holy Spirit is Indispensable

We gratefully acknowledge the permission given by the following Publishers to quote from their copyright publications—

Christian Publications, Inc., Harrisburg, Pennsylvania.
All Nos. except 2, 3, & 12.

Marshall, Morgan & Scott, Ltd., and Oliphants Ltd., London E.C.1.
Nos. 2, 6, & 13.

James Clarke & Co. Ltd., London W.C.1. No. 3

Fleming H. Revell, Co., Westwood, New Jersey.
No. 2

Zondervan Publishing House, Grand Rapids, Michigan. No. 12

Send The Light Trust 1969